A Fire in her Bones

A Fire in her Bones

The Story of Mary Lyon

Dorothy Schack Rosen

 Carolrhoda Books, Inc./Minneapolis

*To the memory of Sydney R. McLean,
extraordinary teacher of my
Mount Holyoke years
and lasting friend.*

Special thanks to Patricia Albright, Assistant Archives Librarian,
Mount Holyoke College Library, and to Clara R. Ludwig.

Carolrhoda Books, Inc. c / o The Lerner Group
241 First Avenue North, Minneapolis, MN 55401

Library of Congress Cataloging-in-Publication Data

Rosen, Dorothy.
    A fire in her bones : the story of Mary Lyon / Dorothy Schack Rosen.
      p. cm.
    Includes bibliographical references and index.
    ISBN 0-87614-840-2 (lib. bdg.)
    1. Lyon, Mary, 1797-1849—Juvenile literature. 2. Mount Holyoke
College—Biography—Juvenile literature. 3. Women college administrators—
United States—Biography—Juvenile literature. 4. Mount Holyoke
College—History—Juvenile literature. [1. Lyon, Mary, 1797-1849.
2. College presidents. 3. Women—Biography. 4. Mount Holyoke
College—History.] I. Title.
LD7092.65.L9R67 1994
378.744'23—dc20   94-1978
                                                            CIP
                                                             AC

Manufactured in the United States of America

1 2 3 4 5 6 – I/JR – 00 99 98 97 96 95

Contents

Mary had fond memories of the house where she was born. She called it "that wild, romantic little farm," but it was a tiny dwelling for a family of ten, with an attic where the children probably slept.

I.

Mary

and the

Hourglass

Mary Lyon stood on tiptoe on a wooden kitchen chair. The little girl was reaching way up to finger the hourglass high on the ledge. Jemima Lyon, Mary's mother, caught her breath as her small daughter swayed. What was the child thinking of? she wondered. Not wanting to frighten the youngster, Jemima tucked her fingers under Mary's arms and swung her down. Chairs were for sitting, not climbing on, Mrs. Lyon reminded her daughter.

But Mary's blue eyes still watched the sand in the hourglass. It kept sifting down. That was how her mother knew when the potatoes were done, since the family didn't own a grandfather clock. The little girl frowned at the hourglass. Her mother was always worrying about time. There never seemed to be enough of it. Couldn't Mary make more time for her mother? the child wondered out loud.

Jemima knelt down and gave the round little form a hug. Then she shook her head in disbelief: If that didn't beat all! Mary wanted to fix the hourglass, to make some more time for me.

Maybe Mary wasn't as handy as the others, with those chubby fingers of hers. But when she grew up, they'd better watch out. Everyone who knew Mary agreed that she never wasted a minute. Why, there'd be no keeping up with her!

Mary Lyon was born on February 28, 1797, part of a big, lively family in a small farmhouse in Buckland, Massachusetts. Mary already had three sisters and a brother, and two younger sisters would come later. Life was not easy on a farm in those years, and even young children had chores to do every day. But the landscape all around them was beautiful, hilly and wild, with a little stream flowing among the rocks.

Because playtime was limited, it was all the sweeter. Young Mary loved racing with her only brother, Aaron, to the top of the steep hill behind their house. Aaron was eight years older, so he was always ahead, but Mary adored him. They would sink down together, panting and laughing, and finally catch their breath. Then they would gaze at the purple line of the far-off mountains that seemed to reach almost to the sunset-streaked sky. How tiny the village looked, way down below, with its peaceful scattering of white houses.

Aaron nearly always managed to have a pocketful of butternuts to share, and they would crack them with a

Mary grew up outside the small town of Buckland, Massachusetts.

big stone and sit there munching. Mary would take a deep lungful of the clear mountain air and giggle with her big brother over nothing.

All too soon it was time to get back to their chores. There was always so much to be done on the farm. Besides the planting and harvesting and fruitpicking, food had to be preserved in vast amounts and stored for the long winter. Almost everything the family wore or used had to be made by hand, even the cradle for the baby.

Most of their cloth was handmade, too. Mary watched the flax being harvested by her father and brother. She peered into the barn when they beat, separated, and combed the tough fibers. Then her mother wound the linen threads on the spinning wheel that she turned with a foot pedal. Jemima Lyon spun the yarn into rolls called knots. The weaker part of the flax threads had to be boiled in ashes and water to make it soft.

Mary and her sisters helped their mother take these rolls to the brook to rinse out the ashes. The chilly water made their hands so red and cold that they had to blow on them and rub them together. Finally the girls took the threads to the loom to weave into cloth.

The two oldest girls, Electa and Jemima, were so good at sewing that Mary despaired of ever being their equal. Their needles seemed to flash in and out of the cloth like magic. It was Mary's nature to put her whole heart into everything she did, and she tried her best to copy them. Oh, the time it took to do all that stitching by hand! Sometimes Mary's fingers ached from clutching the needle. In spite of using the little silver thimble her father, Aaron, had once brought back all the way from Hartford for her birthday, the needle always seemed to stick her.

Her mother would examine the seams and shake her head over the big, uneven stitches. Mary would heave a sigh, but Jemima would urge her on. Just remember, Mrs. Lyon would tell her, when it's finished, no one will ask you how long it took. They'll just say, oh, how nice that looks! And that's what matters.

Mary would rip out the seam and put all of her energy into doing it over. Sometimes it seemed as if she would never finish. The exciting part came when all that tiresome stitching was done and the garment was ready. A new pinafore! Well, it wasn't exactly new, since it used to be Electa's. Mary had shortened it and taken in the seams herself, so it was as good as new. And her sewing was nearly as good as Electa's or Jemima's.

Farm girls like Mary had to learn every step of preparing home-grown flax—spinning, boiling the yarn, and winding it on a reel—as well as weaving the yarn into fabric.

Making winter clothes was especially important, because winter in Massachusetts could be bitter cold and snowy. Even though Mary's father always cut plenty of wood for the fireplace, the cold winds whistling under the eaves made the children shiver at times.

The first step in preparing cold-weather clothes was to shear the sheep for the wool. Next, the wool had to be cleaned, combed, and spun into yarn. Then came the day for dyeing. Mr. Lyon would go on horseback to fetch blue indigo from the little country store to dye the yarn. Sometimes Mary and her sisters collected peach leaves and strips of birch bark to steep for dye of a different color. When the yarn was colored, it was ready to be woven into fabric on the big loom.

Along with her sisters, Mary learned to spin and to weave. If only she could be as quick and handy as they were! No matter, she would tell herself, she'd get it done, even if it took her twice as long.

Finally Mrs. Lyon and the older girls, including Mary, would sew warm wool clothing to keep them snug all through the long winter. Mary loved the soft scratchiness of her thick wool cape, as she folded it around her and brought the hood snugly over her head and ears. Pretty soon she'd be teaching her two little sisters, Rosina and Freelove, how to make strong wool socks, too.

All Mary's world was to change before her sixth birthday. In December of 1802, her quiet, hardworking father died. The whole family gathered about him at the end, even baby Freelove, only sixteen months old.

Afterward, Mary felt as though a giant fist had taken her heart and wrung it. Wasn't it only a little while ago that Pa was outside splitting giant logs? He was the strongest person in the whole world, she was positive. How could he get sick and leave them, quick as a wink?

Mrs. Lyon told her children that their father was with God now; he was at peace. They still had each other. Together they could run the farm, dividing all the chores. They had always been good children, and Jemima knew she could count on them now to do their part. At any rate, there was no sense in crying. It was the will of God, and not for them to question.

God and religion were part of the family's everyday life. Both parents had often read aloud from the Bible. And children weren't spared talk of death in those days.

Most were familiar with the lines from the New England schoolbook, "Xerxes must die, And so must I." The Lyon children listened to their mother and dried their tears. If she could raise her chin bravely and go about the work of the household, so could they.

Mary missed her father already. Terribly. But without him, there was more work than ever on the farm. She and the others were busy every second. Who had time to sit around and mope?

Besides, Mary had discovered a heaven of her own—school. When she was four years old, she had begun her lessons at the district school. Now that she was nearly six, she was already a star pupil. The school was about a mile away from where the Lyons lived. It was a long walk, but Mary didn't mind. Going to school was the most exciting thing that had ever happened to her. She had heard her sisters and brother talking about it, but it was even better than she had expected.

In some towns, girls were allowed to go to school only in the summertime, while boys worked in the fields. In winter, all the girls could do was sit on the doorstep and listen to the boys recite their lessons. But Buckland girls were luckier. They had the same privileges as boys. Mary was glad she lived in Buckland.

The school was a single room, crammed with boys and girls of different ages sitting on rough wooden benches. The big boys and girls sat in the back. There were few books, so they had to be returned to the teacher at once. Paper was scarce, but pupils had slates to write on with chalk. Mary and the others learned reading, grammar,

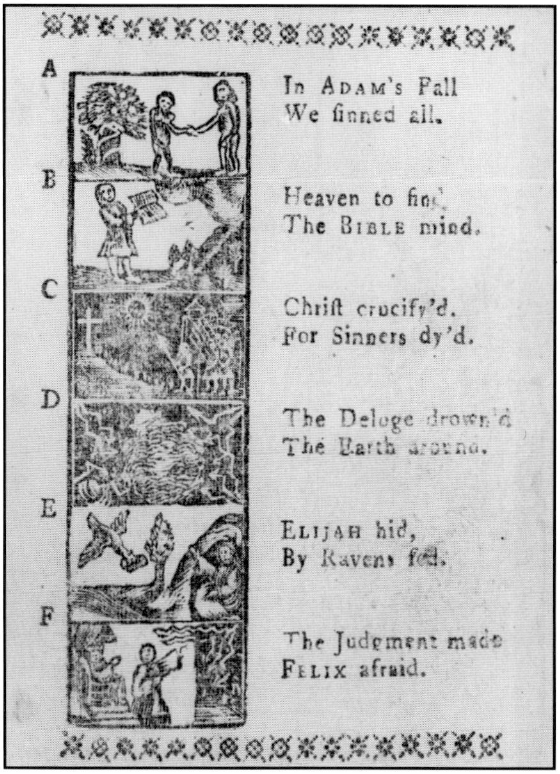
A
In ADAM's Fall
We sinned all.
B
Heaven to find,
The BIBLE mind.
C
Christ crucify'd,
For Sinners dy'd.
D
The Deluge drown'd
The Earth around.
E
ELIJAH hid,
By Ravens fed.
F
The Judgment made
FELIX afraid.

The New England Primer, a book for schoolchildren in the early days of the United States, was filled with references to the Bible.

and arithmetic. The teacher assigned different lessons to groups, from beginners to older pupils. One at a time, boys and girls were called up to the front desk to recite the lesson each had to memorize.

For Mary, discovering the world of school and books was like entering fairyland. She had a wonderful memory and she studied hard. Being called up by the teacher didn't scare her at all. In fact, she was in such a hurry to recite everything that she often spoke too fast. (Some people claimed it hurt to listen to her.) Her words spilled out pell-mell, and the teacher had to hold up a hand and remind her to slow down a bit.

Mary's cheeks would grow pink, and she would take a deep breath and start over. It was easy for her to remember the rules of grammar and arithmetic and to recite whole pages. Spelling matches were the best part of school for Mary, because she could always picture just how the words looked on the page.

When Mary was seven years old, the teacher announced that the school would be moving to another town farther away. Mary came home in tears. How on earth would she ever get that far? She couldn't stop going to school, she just couldn't!

Jemima stroked her daughter's thick red hair and reminded Mary that the Lord would provide a way. What if Mary stayed with her aunt in Ashfield? Of course, Mary would have to pay for her board by helping out in the house and doing as much as she could. It would mean getting up by five o'clock in the morning to put on the kettle or make the biscuits.

Mary's thoughts went back and forth like a seesaw. Could she really do it, leave Ma and Aaron and everyone? She had always loved visiting her aunts and cousins. But to live with them? The school term lasted for months, so she would be coming home only on weekends. And if it snowed hard, not even then. Mary knew it would be awful at first, without her own family to come home to. But she wouldn't quit going to school. No matter what.

When she was especially lonely, Mary would go to the green hills near her home and pray. Years later when she spoke of this time, she said, "My father and mother forsook me, but the Lord took me in."

II.

Forsaken

In 1804 Mary began to spend each school term with a family living close to the district school. Sometimes school was held in the outskirts of Buckland, sometimes in Ashfield. Nearly always Mary stayed with relatives, where she did her best to earn her keep by helping around the house.

She was healthy, lively, and used to hard work on a farm. Families were glad to have Mary in their midst. Though she wasn't naturally handy, she made up for it by putting her whole heart into every task. As one friend said of Mary, "She could make a batch of bread or a tin of biscuit without wasting a dust of flour." She could spin, dye, weave, and embroider as well. And she enjoyed helping the little ones learn their first arithmetic lessons. Still, when the term ended, she was happy to go back home.

When Mary was eleven, things began to change in her family. Her oldest sister, twenty-three-year-old Electa, had become a teacher in the district schools. Now she was marrying and going with her new husband to start a home in New Marlborough, in the southwestern part of Massachusetts. The simple wedding was exciting. To hug Electa good-bye, though, was hard for Mary. New Marlborough was a long way off, with travel by horse and carriage. When would they ever see Electa again?

More changes were to come. Mary's mother was a thrifty manager, and Aaron had always worked hard to make up for the absence of their father. But the struggle became even harder with everyone growing up. The two older girls, Jemima and Lovina, left to become helpers in nearby farmhouses. Both married soon.

Only five sat at the supper table at the Lyon farm now. For Mary, home wasn't the same without her older sisters—even if they did make fun of her just because she put her skirt on inside out a few times. Rosina, age eleven, and Freelove, age nine, were still at home. At thirteen, Mary was the big sister now, and she liked the feeling, but it didn't last long.

One evening Mary's mother called all of the children to sit close to her near the fireplace. Her voice was quiet, but her cheeks seemed flushed. Her eyes searched each face in turn. She was going to be married again, she told them. To a farmer from Ashfield, named Jonathan Taylor. His wife had died and left him with five little girls. He was a hard worker and a good Christian, Jemima explained. He would be a father to all of them.

Mary felt as if her heart had turned to a lump of ice, spreading chills all through her. A strange father? Five strange girls? She remembered her own father's face and the way his eyes shone as he sat by the fireplace, reading to them from the Bible. What would this new father be like?

Mary's mother told the children the rest of the news. Mr. Taylor's house was very small. Only Rosina and Freelove would be going there with her. Aaron would stay to manage the farm. And he would need someone to take care of the house. Mrs. Lyon looked straight at Mary.

In a matter of days, Mrs. Lyon, now Mrs. Taylor, was gone, along with Rosina and Freelove. Aaron was busy from dawn to dusk with farm work. And Mary was busy keeping house. She was so busy, in fact, that there was no time for lessons. Mary's school days seemed to be over, maybe for good. She tried not to be downhearted. She had managed to stay in school past her thirteenth birthday, longer than many girls she knew. But she missed that crowded schoolhouse with all her heart.

Luckily there was plenty for her to do at home, cooking in the open fireplace and baking bread in the brick oven. Besides the washing and the weaving, she had to churn the butter and make the soap and candles.

But working all by herself, hour after hour, was quite a different matter from doing it alongside her mother and sisters. She tried singing the familiar old hymns they sang at church on Sunday. Did the sound echo, or was that just her imagination?

At first Mary cried herself to sleep at night, muffling the sound in her coverlet so Aaron wouldn't hear. The days seemed to stretch ahead endlessly. But Mary was a strong and healthy girl. Soon she was so tired by bedtime, when the last candle was put out, that sleep came easily. And when the first rooster crowed, she would wake up feeling ready for anything. Aaron was going to be proud of her. She would keep the house shining, just the way Ma did.

There were few tools to make Mary's chores easier. Before stoves were common, bread and biscuits were baked in cast-iron bake kettles set on the coals. Housekeeping meant hours of hard labor.

When the emptiness of the little house was too much to bear, Mary would throw on her woolly cloak and step outside. There were the hills, spread out before her. What was it the Psalms called them, "the skipping hills"? Mary would take a deep breath of the clear country air. "I will lift up mine eyes unto the hills, from whence cometh my help," she would recite to herself. "He that keepeth thee will not slumber." Feeling comforted, she would go back indoors, humming a tune.

Aaron comforted Mary too. Every Saturday night after the supper dishes were cleared away, he would hand Mary a silver dollar to pay her for the work she had done. She would thank him and drop the silver piece into the little brown drawstring bag she had made years before from scraps of leftover cloth. Those silver dollars were her hope. She added them to the small inheritance from her father's estate. The money could buy her what she wanted most in the world—to keep on going to school.

Just two years after Mary and Aaron had begun to work on the farm together, he brought home a bride. At first Mary was worried. What would she do if they no longer wanted her to stay there? She was barely fifteen. But Aaron's young wife, Armilla, away from her own home for the first time, was only too glad to have company. And when the babies came, three in quick succession, Mary's strength and household skills were a blessing.

Mary no longer felt alone and forsaken, for Armilla and the children were like a new family and best friends all rolled into one. But sometimes in the evening when the work was done, Mary longed for more books to read than the family Bible. She counted her silver dollars and wondered if, one day, she might have the chance to learn more.

Not long after Mary's seventeenth birthday, a surprising offer came her way. Mary's reputation as an outstanding student had spread beyond Buckland. Even though she had no special training, she was asked to teach for the summer session in the nearby village of Shelburne Falls. At that time, it was hard to get experienced teachers to fill the country schools, and some even younger than Mary were hired.

Her pupils in the district school would also be young, ranging from about four to ten years of age. Her starting salary would be seventy-five cents a week with board. Not nearly as much as a man would make in the same job, and skimpy, even for a young woman in 1814. All the same, this summer job would add to Mary's little pile of savings. And it would put her back in the world of school, the world she loved best. Mary was so excited by the offer that she could hardly sleep. To stand at the head of the schoolroom and be in charge of everything!

Mary Lyon could hardly wait to start teaching.

III.

Star Pupil

That first summer of teaching wasn't as glorious as Mary had imagined. She had to live with the families of her pupils and stay an equal amount of time with each family in turn. Since there were only five students at first, she spent just five days at each home, "boarding 'round." Having to move constantly, even with her few belongings, was a nuisance. And then, there were a lot of rainy days. Rainy weather meant that the bigger boys in the village, unable to work in the fields, would tramp in to join her class.

Suddenly, like all new teachers, Mary had to face problems of discipline. She tried to stand very tall and wear her most severe expression. But whispering would start behind her back while she was busy with the youngest students. Then a pebble hidden in a pocket might fly through the air. Soon Mary had to stop fistfights. By the time the commotion was over, it wasn't easy to restore order. Even the best pupils forgot what they were supposed to be reciting.

This typical classroom in the 1800s shows the challenges Mary had to face as a new teacher. Mary found it so hard to keep order in a classroom filled with youngsters of all ages that she almost gave up teaching.

Mary began to despair. To think that she'd dreamed of being the perfect teacher! Guiding the minds of young angels! The days always started quietly, all eyes on her as she took the roll. But day after day, mischief would crop up. She grew to hate the sight of rain, much as she knew the crops needed it.

One Sunday after church, she heard two farmers' wives talking. "No, Mary Lyon's not the teacher her sister Electa was," one said to the other. Mary's face flamed, and she wondered if the summer would ever end.

Yet, in spite of herself, there were wonderful moments. When she had finally explained an arithmetic problem so her students understood, everything became worthwhile. If only she could keep order all the time!

The long winter gave her plenty of time to think things over. In February she had her eighteenth birthday. Looking back, she decided that maybe she had exaggerated the problems in the classroom. On the whole, she asked herself, wasn't it pretty satisfying? It was the world of school, the best world of all. No, she wasn't ready to give up teaching. Not yet, anyway. If others could do it, why couldn't she?

Meanwhile, whenever she had the chance, she talked to experienced teachers to learn the tricks of the trade. In the summer of 1815, Mary taught once more at the district school. Maybe there were fewer rainy days, or maybe she was learning how to cope. During the next few years, teaching the summer session at Buckland or Ashfield became a regular part of her life.

But Mary still hoped for more. She still dreamed of

the day when she could go back to school as a student and learn all the things she had missed keeping house for Aaron. In the meantime, she hoarded every penny.

Just after Mary turned twenty, she heard that a new private school, Sanderson Academy, was to open in Ashfield. Unlike a district school, an academy could pick and choose the most qualified applicants. The teachers had often had advanced training. If they were men, they might even have gone to college. The subjects they taught ranged far beyond reading and writing.

When Mary heard that the head teacher at Sanderson, Elijah Burritt, would be teaching advanced mathematics and astronomy, she knew she would have to find some way to enroll. Astronomy! Mary knew what the word meant, but she had never before had the chance to study it, or any other science. She was hungry for that chance. Sanderson Academy promised a feast of learning.

Though it took all of her savings to pay for tuition, Mary enrolled at the academy as a student. When it came time to pay for a room in a boardinghouse and a place at the table, Mary found someone willing to take two blue-and-white bedspreads and some table linens she had woven in exchange.

It was worth it. The whole atmosphere at Sanderson made Mary feel more alive than ever. Charged with enthusiasm, she plunged wholeheartedly into her studies. The others at the boardinghouse eyed her with amazement. The gossip around Ashfield was that Mary slept only four hours a night, because she couldn't bear to stop studying!

Sometimes Mary worried that the other students would dislike her, because she studied so hard and recited so often. But she had so much to learn, how could she waste a minute? Eventually her teacher, Mr. Burritt, found himself hard-pressed to keep Mary from getting too far ahead of the others. One Friday he gave her Adams's *Latin Grammar* as an extra assignment to keep her busy. Since she had to keep up with her regular classes as well, he probably felt certain that Mary would have plenty to do.

On Monday Mr. Burritt asked her what she had learned from the Adams book, thinking that she had barely begun on it. In her own rapid-fire way, Mary began to recite. As the minutes passed, everyone turned to stare at her. There was no stopping her. She went on and on. By the time she finished, she had recited from memory every section of grammar in the entire book.

The whole village buzzed with the news of Mary's accomplishment. When someone at the boardinghouse congratulated her, however, she turned red. It seemed that Mary had studied all day Sunday, the Lord's day. The Sabbath was to be spent at church or in Bible study or meditation. Wasn't it wrong, Mary asked herself, to have enjoyed schoolwork on a Sunday? But how could she resist picking up that Latin grammar? Latin was the language of educated people, and a teacher should know it. Mary had never had a chance to learn it before. But she did feel guilty.

Though Mary was in a hurry to learn everything under the sun as fast as she could, she also found time to make a close friend. Amanda White was the lively, brown-haired daughter of Thomas White of Ashfield and his warmhearted wife. Amanda was just the same age as Mary and also excited about attending the academy. They took to each other instantly, their chatter bubbling along without stopping.

Amanda White

When Amanda brought Mary home to her family's big white house, her father and mother were delighted with her bright and eager new friend. Though they had seven children younger than Amanda, the Whites treated Mary as one of their own.

Mary found in them the support she lacked from her mother and stepfather. Mr. Taylor thought Mary already had more than enough schooling. Jemima Lyon Taylor loved her daughter, but she wouldn't think of opposing her husband.

The White family of Ashfield welcomed Mary into their home.

When Mary had no money for the second semester, it was Mr. White who came to her rescue. He used his influence as a trustee of Sanderson Academy to let her stay on free of charge. The Whites also invited her to live with them and share Amanda's room.

For Mary it was a whole new way of life. The sprawling two-story house with the green shutters was a mansion to her. The furniture was polished, the floors had fine carpets. The White house overflowed with life, and Mary felt again how wonderful it was to be back in the midst of a big family.

But Mary was worried, too. Were her manners really good enough? she wondered. At table she watched how the others handled knives and forks. Amanda was so graceful, never dropping a bit of food. She never had a hair out of place on her head, either.

Finally Mary found the courage to ask if Amanda would mind giving her some hints. Amanda was delighted to be asked. They would start with her appearance.

Mary had a marvelous complexion, Amanda told her, so clear and fresh. And big blue eyes, and that thick auburn hair. Perhaps Mary needed to brush her hair more, so it wouldn't fly about so. Maybe they could try pulling it back a bit, to make it smoother.

Mary sat stock-still while Amanda worked on her hair. All her life, she had been in such a rush. When she was growing up on the farm, there was always so much to do. There had never been time to fuss with a hairdo. Ma saw to it that they were clean and had warm clothes in winter. And that was that.

When Mary's hair was finally under control, she looked up at her friend. Would Amanda please correct her if she put on her collar backward? Or forgot to put it on at all? Amanda laughed and then solemnly promised that they would have an inspection every time they left their room.

Mary tried to brush her hair the way Amanda showed her. And scrub the ink spots from her fingers. She also began to hang up her clothes more carefully, as Amanda did, and shake out her cape when she took it off. Mary never wanted to be a lady of fashion, or anything like that. But if she was going to be a better schoolteacher, she should set a better example.

When she had learned all that Sanderson Academy had to teach her, Mary left Ashfield. It was hard for her to say good-bye to Amanda and the Whites. Still, she was happy to go home to Aaron and Armilla and see how the three little children had grown. But her brother's news was a shock.

Aaron had been working as hard as he possibly could, and that was still not hard enough. He could not make a living on the rocky soil of New England. Aaron was selling the farm to buy green and fertile land in western New York State.

Mary had learned to overcome many problems, but this was different. New York State was very sparsely settled, and Mary knew there were no academies in the western part of the state. New England was the only place she could hope to get more education. Even though both Aaron and Armilla begged her to go with them, Mary said no. She couldn't leave New England for the wilderness, not now when she still had so much to learn.

IV.

New Horizons

Sanderson Academy had opened Mary's eyes to new fields. Now, teaching at the district summer school in Buckland, she was eager to introduce a brand-new subject, geography. She had been fired with enthusiasm for it at Sanderson.

The pupils seemed to catch her excitement at learning about the world they were living in. As she watched their stubby fingers carefully drawing maps of the twenty-three states, Mary felt a thrill of satisfaction. What a wonderful feeling, she thought, to be able to pass on what she'd learned!

She could smile now, thinking of that first summer of teaching, when she had sworn never to teach again. But there was so much more for her to learn in order to be a capable teacher. What was it Amanda said about her,

At Amherst Academy, young men and women took the equivalent of modern high school classes.

that Mary was "gaining knowledge by handfuls"? Well, she had to. Every minute counted. After all, she was twenty-one years old already.

In the fall of 1818, Mary decided to spend part of the small sum of money she had received from her father's estate. With it, she enrolled at Amherst Academy, where young women were admitted along with men. The pleasant, tree-lined town of Amherst was some miles to the south, across the Connecticut River. Mary was delighted to be having classes in chemistry, a subject many schools considered too difficult for girls. She snatched up the chance to study the elements and chemical properties, because she knew how rare such opportunities were for women.

The following spring came the news she had been dreading. Aaron and Armilla were ready for the move to western New York. With the first warm weather, the couple with their four children prepared to set out in their covered wagon. The tiny baby's cradle was slung like a hammock from the top of the wagon.

Mary loved them all so much, but she couldn't find the words to tell them. Instead, she thrust a poem she had copied in her best handwriting into Armilla's hand. Armilla nodded and read the New England verse, with its stern message that each person must bear suffering without complaining:

> *Not one sigh shall tell my story,*
> *Not one tear my cheek shall stain;*
> *Silent grief shall be my glory,*
> *Grief that stoops not to complain.*

All too soon it was time for parting. The Lyons climbed up to the wagon seat and waved their good-byes. Aaron turned his head and shouted to the lead wagon. Two other families were leaving, so at least the Lyons would have company. The wagons creaked down the dusty road, and the children waved until they were out of sight.

Strangers would be coming soon, probably that very day, to take possession of the Lyon family farm. The farmhouse was the only real home Mary had ever known. She no longer even had a permanent address. And she could no longer come running home to Aaron. Would she ever have a home of her own again? she wondered.

When Mary finished the summer term in Buckland, she found work teaching for the winter in a nearby town. Soon she was teaching almost continuously, moving from one town to another as the season changed. She was supporting herself and even saving a few pennies. Every bit she saved would buy her the chance to study more.

Mary knew it would be difficult to find more advanced studies. Up to now, she had attended district schools and academies where boys studied as well as girls. After graduating from an academy, a young man could go on to college. But a young woman didn't have that choice, even one as smart as Mary Lyon. Some female seminaries offered more training, but in the 1820s they were few and far between.

When Mary was twenty-four, she heard from Amanda White about a fine seminary for young ladies recently opened at Byfield, one hundred miles away. The seminary was more advanced than any school Mary had attended up to now. Mary decided to enroll there with Amanda, even though her family and friends argued against her going so far.

Amanda and Mary rode in Mr. White's big carriage while he held the reins. The trip to the northeastern corner of Massachusetts took three days, and they got lost on the way. Amanda couldn't stop crying, she was so frightened and homesick.

Mary tried to cheer her up, but with night coming on, she grew tearful herself. She was using up all her savings, as well as the last of her share from her father's estate. Her stepfather had at first refused to let her have her own money. Had she made a mistake, Mary wondered, investing every penny she owned to go to this faraway school?

Mary remembered the teacher, Joseph Emerson, more than the building at Byfield Seminary. Unlike many men of his day, Emerson thought that women were as intelligent as men.

But once in Byfield, Mary was thrilled with all she learned there. Joseph Emerson, the principal and head teacher, believed firmly that young women deserved the best in education. He even went so far as to predict that one day soon "female institutions, very greatly superior to the present, will not only exist, but be considered as important, as are now our colleges for the education of our sons."

Emerson's views were so far ahead of the times as to be shocking. The very idea that women could seek higher education sent chills of excitement up Mary's spine. Only men could attend Harvard or Yale or similar colleges. Colleges for women did not exist. And most people—men and women alike—thought that was how things should be.

After all, they argued, what good would an education do a woman? It wouldn't help her keep house, they said. And it wouldn't make her a better cook or mother.

Mr. Emerson's assistant, Zilpah Grant, seemed to be living proof of what good an education could do a woman. Zilpah was a striking young woman from Connecticut, intelligent and lively. She was only a few years older than Mary and was as excited about teaching as Mary was.

Like Mary, she had lost her father early in life. Her mother, too, had remarried. Zilpah was teaching in a district school even before her fifteenth birthday. She had argued with relatives, just as Mary had, about spending all her inheritance and savings to attend Mr.

Zilpah Grant

Emerson's school at Byfield. Mr. Emerson had been so impressed with her ability that he had made her his assistant.

Mary and Zilpah became fast friends almost at once. They spent hours discussing everything from chemistry to fashion to schooling for women. Zilpah too was inspired by Mr. Emerson's suggestion that a true college, more permanent than his own seminary, would one day open its doors to women.

Mary had seen schools for young ladies come and go. Some lasted a term or two, some lasted a decade. But even when some outstanding teacher (often a woman) opened a seminary for young ladies, it usually closed after a few years from lack of funds.

What was needed was a permanent institution, a school that might outlast its founders. Only when permanent schools for women existed could farm girls like Mary hope to gain an education without constant struggling.

All too soon the session at Byfield ended. But Mary's gamble paid off. Almost at once, she received an offer to come back to Sanderson Academy as preceptress, or assistant to the principal. At first the male principal, a Dartmouth College graduate, was doubtful about hiring a female for the position. Finally, at the urging of Amanda White's father, he agreed to try her. The zest that Mary brought to her work soon convinced the principal. She was invited to stay on.

The following year she was surprised by a visit from her brother Aaron. He had come all the way from western New York to persuade his favorite sister to go

Mary returned to Sanderson Academy not as a student but as the assistant to the principal.

back there with him. Teachers were very scarce on the frontier, and there was a great need to be filled. Mary could have her choice of jobs. Aaron and Armilla and the little ones missed her terribly.

Would she make her home with them again? Aaron asked. Would she come? She had had enough schooling by now, surely.

Mary could hardly sleep. Going to New York State would mean seeing Aaron, Armilla, and the children. But to leave the post she had now at Sanderson Academy would be a terrible wrench. She had worked so hard to get this far. And she could not forget the words of Joseph Emerson. If there was going to be a real college for young women, as he predicted, she was certain that it would be in New England. Mary had to say no to Aaron again, but she wondered if she was making the right decision.

The following summer, while Sanderson was closed, Mary taught at a school in Conway. She was able to board at the home of a young minister, Edward Hitchcock, and his wife, Orra. Mary knew and liked Orra, who had taught at Amherst Academy while Mary was a student there.

Here was an opportunity Mary had no intention of wasting. While boarding with the Hitchcocks, she managed to study science with the minister and drawing with Orra. Mary thought herself lucky to be around two people so chock-full of talent and so willing to spend their time teaching her. She felt even luckier when the Hitchcocks, drawn to Mary's warm open ways, became her friends as well as her teachers.

During a vacation from teaching, Mary found learning and friendship at the home of Professor Edward Hitchcock. From Orra Hitchcock, who made this sketch of South Hadley Falls, Massachusetts, Mary learned to draw and paint.

Edward Hitchcock

The following year, Mary spent her time between terms attending lectures in chemistry and natural history given by the famous Amos Eaton. Mary had written to him at Rensselaer Polytechnic Institute in Troy, New York, where he was the principal. In her letter, she had told him about the problems she was having in teaching chemistry. Professor Eaton generously invited her to come to Troy and stay with his family. Mary was able to attend classes in physics and chemistry, normally open only to men, and she got extra help from Professor Eaton himself.

When she thought of all that she had learned in the past few years, Mary knew that she had been right not to go west with Aaron. What chances would she have had to improve herself out there in the wilderness? she asked herself. She had had such a wonderful time, staying with the Hitchcocks and the Eatons. Studying with an expert like Amos Eaton was a joy. There was so much more that she could teach now.

One day a letter arrived with a surprise. Zilpah Grant was inviting Mary to come and teach with her at a brand-new female academy to be opened in Londonderry, or Derry, New Hampshire. Zilpah was to be the principal of Adams Female Academy, and she was positive that Mary was just the right person to help her.

Mary's heart must have thumped when she put down the letter. What on earth was she to do? Could she really leave Sanderson? They had given her the chance she had needed. Wouldn't it be wrong to turn her back on them?

Answering Zilpah, Mary wrote, "After breaking the seal of your letter, and eagerly running over the contents, said I, 'Is this a dream, or a sober reality?'"

Wasn't the need for her help greater in a new place? Mary asked herself. Or did she want to go to New Hampshire just to work alongside Zilpah? Finally, she agreed to join her friend. She couldn't turn her back on the excitement of starting a whole new school.

V.

Beginnings

Mary was not disappointed with Adams Female Academy. In April 1824, she traveled to Derry to become one of the three teachers assisting Zilpah. Mary was paid five dollars a week plus board for the term, which lasted thirty weeks.

In spite of the fact that Zilpah was Mary's employer, the friendship between the two seemed only to grow stronger. Zilpah had such a magnetic personality that both the teachers and the students admired and imitated her. (Many years later a magazine article reported only half jokingly that European visitors came to the United States to see Niagara Falls and Zilpah.)

But where Mary was sturdy and healthy, Zilpah was frail. When both Mary and Zilpah came down with typhoid fever one summer, Zilpah became so ill that Mary was afraid she'd die. Zilpah got better slowly. Mary herself bounced back quickly and then did the work of two. She lost much of her hair and joked later that she hoped to "continue to have enough to support my combs." (No woman takes the loss of her hair lightly, but Mary wasn't one to spend time complaining. She simply wore a cap or turban from that time on.)

Mary and Zilpah's very differences proved helpful. Mary was the comic, always ready with a joke, often about herself. Zilpah had a flair for fashion. Mary appealed to her often for advice on her wardrobe. How should last year's spring bonnet be trimmed to give it a new look? Zilpah knew at once and went along to guide Mary's shopping. And when it was time to make a summer dress, Zilpah helped Mary choose the nine yards of gingham.

Meanwhile, the school flourished. Mary was surprised to find the plan even superior to that at Byfield. Instead of trying to cover many subjects, at Derry the pupils studied only a few at a time. The subject matter was reviewed over and over. Students were encouraged to ask questions and join in discussions. Even small matters were done with care. To Amanda White, now married and living in Michigan, Mary wrote, "Each pupil, for instance, is required to write with a pen of her own making, and no one is allowed to request any of her mates to make or mend her pen."

The academy demanded hard work from the sixty young women students. They were tested and divided into three classes: junior, middle, and senior. Their ages ranged widely, and the teachers didn't always find it easy to instruct young women whose earlier schooling differed greatly.

At Adams Female Academy in Derry, New Hampshire, Mary learned firsthand how to run a large school.

From her first days in the one-room schoolhouse, Mary had had a hard time keeping order. But Zilpah had a scheme to end unruly behavior. Mary, full of admiration, wrote to Hannah White, Amanda's sister. "Miss G[rant] has adopted a plan to prevent [whispering]," Mary reported, "which has been very successful. After leading her pupils to feel the importance of being truthful, and stating facts as they are, she requires each to bring in a weekly ticket with her name attached, stating whether she has, or has not, made any communication in school during the week, either by whispering, or by writing..." Mary liked this honor system because she felt that self-reporting helped the students feel grown-up and responsible.

Adams Female Academy was in session only from spring through fall, since the winters in Derry were harsh. As soon as Mary went back to Buckland in the autumn of 1824, she was invited to start a winter school for girls. Mr. Clark, the minister who made the offer, also invited Mary to board with his family.

She could run a three-month winter school in her old neighborhood, Mr. Clark explained, while continuing to work during the rest of the year with Zilpah. Mary was twenty-seven years old, blazing with plans for everything she wanted to do. It took her weeks of hard work to organize her own school, but all the effort was worthwhile. At last she was beginning to accomplish what she had dreamed of. She was educating ordinary girls like herself, young middle-class women who could not afford to attend expensive private academies.

This inside view of the lecture hall at a seminary for women from the 1870s is probably similar to classrooms at Adams.

Mary's first winter school had twenty-five girls. Problems arose with keeping order, but Mary borrowed Zilpah's plan. Some of the students resisted the honor system at first, but soon each girl had pledged not to whisper or write notes. Writing compositions, too, brought a tug-of-war. As Mary wrote to a teacher friend, "One pupil refused entirely to write." Eventually Mary managed to convince this stubborn one to put pen to paper.

Mary did so well that she soon had ninety-nine pupils and two assistant teachers to help her. One of Mary's goals was to prepare young women to teach. Besides a thorough grounding in arithmetic, grammar, and geography, she gave her students lessons in how to get along in the classroom. She tried to make her students catch some of her own excitement about teaching. "Make the dull ones think once a day," she advised the teachers-to-be. "Make their eyes sparkle once a day!"

Word of Mary's program spread quickly, and many visitors came to study her methods. Teachers were needed in schoolrooms everywhere, and school committees sent members to Mary's school to hire her best pupils to teach in their districts. Mary's work was known and respected.

Early in 1828 while Mary was in Buckland, Zilpah wrote that she was leaving Adams Academy. The trustees had voted to add music and dancing to the curriculum. Zilpah wanted no connection with "finishing schools" where rich young women were taught the "social graces."

In a short time, Zilpah would be ready to open a school more to her liking, and she begged Mary to join her.

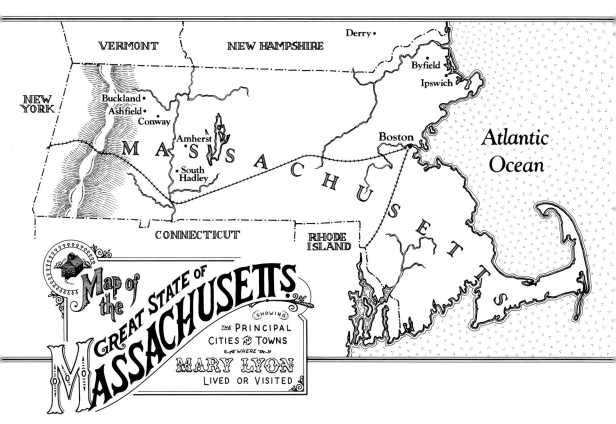

This school would be located at Ipswich, on the Massachusetts coast. And it would be open year-round. To join her friend, Mary would have to close her own school.

Give up the winter school? Mary had worked so hard to make it a success. She had done it all by herself.

Ipswich was in the far northeastern corner of Massachusetts, a long way from Buckland and Mary's friends and family. Though Mary had been separated at a young age from her mother and sisters, she cared for them deeply. She worried especially about her sister Lovina. Just as Mary was trying to decide whether to go to Ipswich, Lovina's husband, Daniel, took sick and died.

Lovina became ill and never fully recovered. Freelove, Mary's youngest sister, took care of Lovina's five little children while Mary paid all the bills from her slender savings. Would she be able to continue to help if she accepted a job in faraway Ipswich?

And what would become of the young women who wanted to study at her winter school? So many schools for girls closed when the teacher lost interest or moved on. Mary knew many of her students could not afford to go to the distant, more expensive school at Ipswich. When news spread that Mary might give up the winter school, a group of nearby ministers begged her to stay.

That winter Mary wrote long letters to Zilpah discussing whether it was right for her to leave Buckland, where schools were so scarce. Zilpah wrote back, "I have considered your assistance and friendship among my greatest earthly blessings." Could Mary say no to Zilpah's invitation?

Still, for months Mary could not make up her mind. Finally she agreed to go. She would start in April 1830. In addition to teaching, she was to be assistant principal. She told Zilpah she would teach for two years. After that, she would see if she wanted to stay on. By then she would know if Ipswich was the school she had been dreaming about.

This miniature portrait, painted on ivory when she was thirty-five, is the earliest known picture of Mary. Such miniatures were popular before photography was invented. Mary exchanged miniatures with Zilpah and other close friends.

VI.

Bonds of Friendship

When Mary traveled to Ipswich that spring, she was a healthy, vigorous young woman. Friends often spoke of her big blue eyes, her liveliness, and her "wonderfully expressive face."

Her friend Eunice Caldwell, who taught with her, claimed that in the summer of 1830, Mary received "a tempting offer which she thought held out as good a prospect of a life of love and happiness as any she could expect." The offer was a proposal of marriage. No one knows why Mary "gave the final negative," as Eunice put it, and refused the man's offer. In Mary's many lengthy letters, she never mentioned this love affair.

Why did Mary turn down this chance to marry? Perhaps she measured possible suitors against her brother, Aaron, so that none was worthy. Or perhaps the proposal was simply not attractive enough for Mary to give up her career. Married women did not usually work outside the home then. Nearly all of the young women teachers Mary knew had given up their own careers when they married.

By fall Mary was immersed in the daily routine at Ipswich. The school soon grew to have 191 pupils. Zilpah depended on Mary to supervise the living arrangements of the students, who were scattered in different rooming houses. Often roommates could not get along with each other, and then it was up to Mary to find pleasing partners for each. Sometimes she had to make several switches to get the right match.

It was difficult to find enough boardinghouses in the town as the school grew. Eventually Zilpah and Mary decided not to accept pupils under fourteen. That would make Mary's job of finding rooms easier. And it would limit classes to students who were well prepared.

The catalogue stated that entering students were expected to "be skilful in both mental and written Arithmetic, and thoroughly acquainted with Geography and the History of the United States." The courses at Ipswich were based on the new idea of emphasizing English, mathematics, and the sciences. In her chemistry classes, Mary did actual experiments, which she had learned from Professor Eaton. Such teaching was rare in men's colleges in the 1830s. In a female seminary, it was unheard-of.

Almost from the first, Mary and Zilpah found places for their graduates to teach. Mary wrote to school principals and teachers all over the country searching for openings. She took great care to recommend the young woman best suited for a particular position. Who knew better than Mary the woes a young teacher faced in a strange town? Mary's former students wrote back with tales of their teaching and living conditions. In this way, Mary learned what was going on in schoolrooms everywhere and could better prepare the young women at Ipswich.

In the autumn of 1831, Zilpah's health problems forced her to leave the school. She went to Georgia to rest and recover. Mary now took full charge of Ipswich Seminary. In addition to teaching classes, solving housing problems, training assistant teachers on the staff, and finding jobs for graduates, she now had to keep track of finances. She even managed to take over Zilpah's Bible classes.

The seminary building at Ipswich was solid and imposing, but it didn't belong to the school. Having a permanent building seemed to Mary and Zilpah to be the first step in making schools for women more like those for men.

Mary also found time to work on a plan she and Zilpah had started before Zilpah left. The two of them had been thinking for a long time about starting a school for women that would be more like colleges for men. First of all, the school had to have an adequate laboratory and a library. Next, it needed a dormitory close by, where students could live instead of being scattered in boarding-houses. Most important of all, it had to have the permanent base that kept men's colleges from running out of money. Mary and Zilpah had seen too many women's schools fail from lack of funds.

What kept Harvard and Yale and the other men's colleges running? Each had a permanent endowment. A sum of money had been put aside for the ongoing needs of the college. This sum was kept up by gifts from graduates and friends.

In the months before Zilpah's illness, she and Mary had asked the trustees of Ipswich Female Seminary to consider their plan for a permanently endowed school. Mary and Zilpah weren't sure how the trustees would react. These men were trusted with the affairs of the school, and they might well think that the plan was out-landish. After all, most people didn't think young women needed any more than the basics of reading and writing, let alone an education that would rival that at men's colleges. When the trustees at first agreed to help, Mary and Zilpah had high hopes.

After Zilpah left, however, meetings with the trustees resulted in more and more problems. Still, Mary was en-thusiastic. In February 1832, she wrote to her good friend

Professor Hitchcock of Amherst College asking for his help. That summer she wrote a prospectus, or a draft plan, called "New England Female Seminary for Teachers." But in the fall, by the time her pamphlet had been printed and sent out, no one seemed to show much interest.

Mary tried to maintain her enthusiasm, but she had family sorrows. In September 1832, she received word of the death of her sister Rosina, whose children Mary had been overseeing for some time. A few weeks later, news came that Lovina, too, had died. "My mother has buried two children in one month," she wrote to Zilpah. In spite of these tragedies, Mary continued to push her plan with the same vigor as before. But it was hard going.

In the 1830s, women were not supposed to have anything to do with business matters. A woman's place was in the home, people said, keeping house and taking care of children. Mary realized that if she and Zilpah kept on presenting their plan for a woman's school as their own, it would never succeed. She wrote to Zilpah that their plan had better appear to be the idea of some generous men. A plan backed by women alone would always be laughed at or ignored.

No one knows what Zilpah said in reply, but by early in 1833, Mary knew that the school plan was going nowhere. The trustees did little to help her, and Mary felt that Zilpah was also letting her down. Zilpah had been sick now for more than a year. From the time she left Ipswich, Zilpah had played no part in Mary's efforts to rouse interest in a permanent school. Answering Mary's letters was all she had done. And during all that time, Mary had been carrying the complete burden of running Ipswich Seminary by herself.

That winter Mary wrote to Zilpah stating that she felt her services as assistant principal would no longer be needed after Zilpah's return. "I have thought," Mary wrote, "that there was nothing that we could do together which we could not do separately." Running the school could be done just as well, she wrote, "by one of us."

When Zilpah returned to Ipswich in June 1833, she asked Mary to stay on for another year. Mary reluctantly agreed, but she took the summer off to travel. It was the first vacation she ever had, and she made the most of it. She traveled more than two thousand miles by stagecoach, carriage, steamship, canalboat, and one early, short section of railroad. She gazed at Niagara Falls

On her vacation in the summer of 1833, Mary covered over 2,000 miles to visit schools and wonders like Niagara Falls.

and the Catskill Mountains, visited museums and factories in New York and Philadelphia, and braved the new frontier as far as Detroit. Mary also managed to find time to visit Aaron, Armilla, and their children in western New York State. To Mary's joy, dear Aaron was "the same kind-hearted, generous, affectionate brother."

Everywhere on her travels, Mary went to schools and talked with teachers. She saw the need for trained teachers all over the new country. At the same time, she knew from experience that most young women could not afford to attend seminaries like Ipswich. Where could they find the education they needed?

Mary also knew from experience how young women had to scurry about to get their learning in bits and pieces. In the months before she left Ipswich, she began thinking about founding a permanently endowed school without Zilpah's help. She envisioned a school with "the style plain, the food simple, almost all the labor done by the teachers and scholars, and the expenses very low."

Mary would be leaving her job at Ipswich Seminary at the end of September 1834. Her friends worried that she was giving up a regular salary for a daydream. But Mary had made up her mind. She wrote to her sister Freelove that she was about to "embark in a frail boat on a boisterous sea." Since things had not worked out with Zilpah, Mary would find her way on her own. From now on she could use all her energy for one purpose: to create the school so desperately needed.

VII.

Door-to-Door Crusader

How exactly would Mary's school differ from semi-naries such as Ipswich? First, it would be as permanent as the colleges for men. A board of trustees, not concerned with making a personal profit, would oversee the permanent endowment.

Second, tuition would be kept low so even poor young women could afford to attend. Mary would seek out teachers with a missionary spirit, teachers more interested in doing good than in making money.

Third, the students would not be scattered in boarding-houses as at Ipswich. They would all live together in a dormitory close to the classrooms, two students to a room. To keep costs low, the young women would do the housework. In this way, Mary explained, they would get needed exercise while enjoying each other's company. Doing the chores would also help them form the habit of "working cheerfully for the common good."

In Ipswich, Mary had her first success as a fund-raiser.

On September 6, 1834, just weeks before she left her job, Mary invited a dozen gentlemen to her parlor at Ipswich. They formed a committee to work on Mary's proposal for a school for women. This time, Mary let it be known that the male committee members—not a woman—were behind the proposal. She wasn't going to let prejudices against women stall her plans.

Mary set about raising the first thousand dollars herself. Times were especially hard, and Mary knew that a bold approach was needed. She called on women, in and about Ipswich. She went from house to house, telling them how much more important this school was than "a new shawl." With her usual humor, she convinced husbands to "cut off one little corner of their estates, and give it to their wives to invest in the form of a seminary for young ladies." Mary talked fast! She had an answer for every objection before it was raised.

Mary's glowing words proved persuasive. Soon she had raised nearly all of the first thousand dollars. Raising this sum convinced her male supporters that she could do the job. Of course, much more money was needed. Traveling in other towns, Mary told the women how generous the ladies of Ipswich had been. She also wrote letter after letter to old friends, such as Amanda White's father in Ashfield, and to former teachers, including Professor Hitchcock of Amherst.

Meanwhile Mary needed a place to live. That October she ended her connection with Zilpah Grant's school. Professor Hitchcock and his wife, Orra, solved Mary's problem by inviting her to share their home in Amherst.

From the fall of 1834 on, Mary used Amherst as her base. She traveled far and wide and held meeting after meeting, persuading "benevolent gentlemen" to help her. Mary talked one man, Reverend Roswell Hawks, into getting a leave of absence from his church to raise money. It was a relief not to do all the fund-raising herself.

Some people said Mary's "riding about the countryside with Mr. Hawks to ask for sixpenny contributions" was unladylike. But Mary paid no attention, saying, "I learned twenty years ago never to get out of patience."

Mary's account books show that the residents of ninety-one towns gave a total of $27,000. The largest amounts were two gifts of $1,000 each. The smallest were three gifts of six cents each. The number of tiny contributions shows how hard Mary worked. How many doors she had to knock on, in all kinds of weather, to fill her green-velvet money bag!

Mary wrote in 1836, "Had I a thousand lives, I could sacrifice them all in suffering and hardship for [the school's] sake. Did I possess the greatest fortune, I could easily relinquish it all, and become poor, and more than poor, if its prosperity would demand it."

Daniel Safford

Deacon Daniel Safford of Boston was one of the most generous donors of all. His wife was enthusiastic about the plan for the school. Mary was always welcome at the Saffords' when her travels brought her to Boston.

In spite of the welcome they and other friends gave her, traveling wore Mary down. "I wander about without a home," she wrote her mother, "scarcely knowing one week where I shall be the next." She never knew for certain where her search for funds might take her. "I spent last Wednesday night at Belchertown, Thursday night at Barre, Friday night at Amherst, and yesterday returned here," she told Zilpah in another note. Her friends worried that her hectic workdays were putting a severe strain on her health.

There were other strains as well. Roswell Hawks, now president of the trustees, was beginning to act like the president of the planned school. During one discussion, he snapped at Mary, "I am the head of this institution." But she faced him and declared, "Then I am the neck!"

These were certainly "trying times," as Mary admitted in a letter. But heated meetings with trustees only pushed her to work harder. Different towns vied for the honor of being chosen for the site of the school. Mary left the choice up to the trustees, who eliminated one town after another. Finally, they decided on South Hadley, Massachusetts, after it agreed to raise its pledge from five thousand to eight thousand dollars in just fifteen days.

South Hadley, Massachusetts

Andrew Porter was so impressed by Mary and her plan that he began to spend his entire week overseeing building at South Hadley.

What would the school be called? Mary never wanted it to be named after her. That simply wasn't her style. So many schools made famous by a single teacher had disappeared. Professor Hitchcock wanted the name to be "Pangynaskean," a Greek word for "whole-woman-making." Mary must have held her breath until he was outvoted!

The mountain on the horizon of South Hadley provided the answer. Mount Holyoke Female Seminary was born, in name at least. Soon Mary's dream came a step closer to reality. In February 1836, the school received a charter from the State of Massachusetts. Then in August workers broke ground for the main building, and the cornerstone was laid in October.

During the construction, one part of a brick wall collapsed while the workers were eating breakfast. The foreman worried that Mary would be upset. But she came hurrying over to him, telling him how thankful she was that none of the workmen were injured. The wall was swiftly rebuilt.

Soon the building was nearly finished, but there was no money left at all for furnishings. Mary turned to the people who had always given her the most support. She asked ladies in nearby towns to form clubs. Each club would work to raise enough funds (fifty to sixty dollars) to furnish a student room. If the ladies couldn't send money, then Mary asked for loans or gifts of cutlery, comforters, pillows, and even beds.

Not everyone shared Mary's enthusiasm. Many people made fun of the seminary. The very idea was called "unnatural...unfeminine and anti-Christian." In April 1837, *The Religious Magazine* attacked Mary's plan, denounced women teachers as "masculine," and compared the students' housekeeping chores to slave labor. But Mary went on with the work of fund-raising, confident that her dream would soon be real.

The school was actually under construction. She was not going to let anything or anyone get in her way now. "It has sometimes seemed as if there was a fire, shut up in my bones," Mary explained to a friend. The dream of opening Mount Holyoke Female Seminary made that fire burn even more brightly.

VIII.

$\mathcal{O}$pening the $\mathcal{D}$oors

In August 1837, New York, Boston, and local newspapers advertised the upcoming opening of Mount Holyoke Female Seminary. Two hundred young women applied for admission. Mary sifted through their letters of application and wondered if the building would be ready for them. On September 6, she wrote to her mother, "My head is full of closets, shelves, cupboards, doors, sinks, tables...." Two weeks later, progress was being made, but, she wrote, "Some parts of the paint will be so fresh that we must use it with the greatest care."

Opening day was November 8, 1837. "The doors," Professor Hitchcock wrote, "were without steps; the windows without blinds; the wood-house was not covered; stoves were not set up; the furniture, delayed by storms, had not all arrived; and much of the bedding

When Mount Holyoke Female Seminary opened in 1837, it filled just one building. Each student was required to bring "towels for her own use, one pair of sheets and pillow cases for her bed, and one tablespoon and one teaspoon."

pledged had not made its appearance." Yet in spite of these problems, that day was one of the happiest of Mary Lyon's life.

The sounds of hammers filled the air. But none of the tumult affected Mary's greeting to the girls arriving by coach at the five-story brick building. She met them, a student recalled, with "her face all aglow." "Come right upstairs," Mary called out to them, "you have come to help us!"

The girls did not go hungry, since a table of refreshments had been prepared. From the first moment, they were treated like members of a family, each one given a task to do. One girl, who worried about being away from home, was kept so busy unpacking mattresses, peeling apples, and finishing off quilts that she never had time to become homesick. Meanwhile, girls sitting on piles of mattresses were taking the entrance exams.

That first week, Mary Lyon was up at four o'clock in the morning to supervise the groups tackling the cooking, baking, and dishwashing, as well as the cleaning. Only when all the morning's work was finished could Mary and the other teachers get down to the task of educating the students.

One setback could have been a calamity. Mary had hired Miss Peters, a former teacher at the Byfield school, to oversee the students doing chores. But poor Miss Peters was soon overwhelmed by her task. "Everything seemed like a mountain to her," Mary recalled. Miss Peters left in tears, so Mary had to do her work, too.

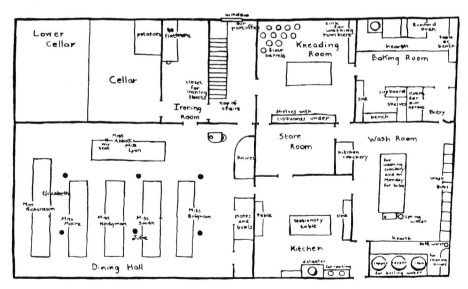

Lucy Goodale, a student at the school, was so impressed by the organization of the seminary's basement that she drew this plan to send home to her family.

She tackled the problem with her usual common sense, picking two "General Leaders" from the students to supervise the others. Then she appealed to the entire student body: "This is an experiment, and I cannot succeed without your help." The young women rose to Mary's expectations.

One student, Nancy Everett, wrote home explaining how it all worked: "Perhaps you may like to know about the division of labor and this I will try to tell you. In the first place, the bell rings at five o'clock in the morning to call up those who get breakfast, which consists of potatoes (very nice) and cream, white bread and butter. Sometimes for variety hasty pudding is substituted for the former. It takes fourteen to get breakfast—eight to set the tables, there being five to set—one to make the fires, in the stove, under the set kettles for dishwater, potatoes and washing floors; and...then five or six to peel the potatoes."

All that hard work, and just to get breakfast! Each student pitched in, and some even enjoyed it. After only two weeks at Mount Holyoke, Nancy Everett concluded, "I believe if ever there was a happy family it is this!"

Still, there were problems to work out in Mary's system. Bread baked in the new Rumford oven, a gift from the Saffords, proved disappointing. For days Mary carried her portable writing desk to the baking room. While she wrote letters, she watched over the rising dough. Finally she and her student bakers were turning out "light, sweet bread."

Nancy Everett was amazed by Mary's energy. "I really do not know when she sleeps," Nancy wrote home, "for she is up the first in the house, sometimes before four, and once she rose at one thinking it was five!" (Nancy knew about the mistake, because Mary had rung the wake-up bell.)

Washday seemed to be dreaded by all. Each Monday students carried pails of hot water from stove to tub in order to scrub and wring all the linens. Mary tried to find a chore to suit each person. To a slender girl ironing tablecloths she said, "You are not strong enough for that work, you must have something lighter." (In the 1830s, irons, which had to be heated on the stove, were very heavy.) Some families of students worried that their daughters might not be strong enough to do servants' work and study at the same time.

Although the chores at Mount Holyoke were hard work, most students were grateful to have been accepted to a school where the tuition and board was only sixty-four dollars a year. "We brought our wood and water from the basement and thought it no hardship," one student wrote. "We were so glad to have a place in the seminary, for we knew that more than twice our number had been refused."

Besides, the students enjoyed the chance to put aside their studies and join a work circle. Some joked about it. "Wednesday (today) is recreation day," one wrote, "but some of the young ladies call it workation day, there is so much to be done."

In March Mary decided to go to Boston for three weeks as a test, so that, as she said, "I might (besides finding a little rest) know whether the wheels which I had been occupied so long in arranging could move without my aid." When she returned, the girls of that first year rushed to greet her. They crowded about her as if she were a long-lost mother. "Everything," Mary was glad to report, "was in perfect order...."

But Mary had set more into motion than just a system of chores. From the beginning, academic standards were high. The school's three-year course of study had a junior, middle, and senior class. No one was admitted under the age of sixteen. The entrance exams showed that many students were ill prepared. Those who couldn't pass any part at all had to leave. A student who failed in some part of the exams had to return home and study that area until she had mastered it.

No student was allowed to take more than three courses at a time. Subject matter was gone over constantly. A student wrote home, "They are very thorough here, more so than I expected. They will make us get our lessons and get them well. I thought I knew something before I came here, but sometimes I feel as if I did not know anything."

Students took courses in mathematics, English, history, philosophy, and the sciences. Mary herself managed to find time to teach both chemistry and physics. But she believed in exercise for the body as well as for the mind. Besides taking exercise classes, each pupil was supposed to take a brisk daily walk in the fresh air. (And in the middle of winter in western Massachusetts, the air was often very fresh and very brisk!)

In August 1838, the first school year was over. Three seniors were qualified enough to graduate. The girls wore white dresses and carried parasols to the graduation ceremony. A procession of trustees, Mary and the other teachers, and then the students paraded from the seminary to the nearby church.

Mary was thrilled with the success of that first year, but she had no time to sit back and enjoy her triumph. She was busier than ever at Mount Holyoke, and she had family sorrows to face again. In 1838 Mary lost her older sister, Jemima. In September 1839, her youngest sister, Freelove, died. Now four sisters were gone, and Electa lived far away in New York State. In November Mary's mother died. This last blow affected her so deeply that she became ill and unable to work for weeks.

Deacon Safford urged her to travel west with him and his wife. Mary agreed, and the trip seemed to restore her health. But just when Mary was feeling better, tragedy struck.

During the nine-week summer vacation in 1840, nine Mount Holyoke students died of typhoid fever. Many others were seriously ill. Had they become infected before the end of the term on July 30? It seemed so. Yet the school was kept spotlessly clean and scrubbed. The talk was that the girls studied too hard and were "kept in too close."

Mary did not believe it. She declared that cleaning standards at the school could not be improved. But in the next year, she emphasized health—a proper diet and good sleep habits, along with daily exercise—more than ever. She also set up an infirmary for the sick and made arrangements for a doctor to be on call.

During the typhoid epidemic in 1840, nine students died and many parents refused to let their daughters return to Mount Holyoke. Lucy Goodale was one of the dead, but her family had enough confidence in Mary Lyon to send Lucy's sisters Mary and Harriet to the school.

In the fall of 1840, after the typhoid epidemic, only 80 of the 120 students returned to Mount Holyoke. Mary went to her waiting list of students, and soon the dormitory rooms were full again—too full, in fact. More room was needed for the many applying for admission. Mary issued an appeal for donations to build more dormitory rooms, as well as for furniture and laboratory equipment. By December 1841, builders finished work on a new south wing.

Over the years, Mount Holyoke grew and prospered. Still, Mary was not satisfied. To a student she confided, "I shall not live to see this a college, but I believe you will live to see the time when girls shall have just as good opportunities as their brothers."

The fame of the school grew, and so did the size of the student body. By 1847 it had grown to about three hundred, and Mary decided to raise the standards for admission. Applicants had to have some knowledge of Latin, which had recently become a requirement for graduation—just as it was in the best colleges for men. Sixteen-year-olds would rarely be admitted. The catalogue stated that "it is generally better that they should not enter under seventeen or eighteen."

The entrance exams were made more difficult to screen out candidates who were not prepared. In 1847, after taking the exams, Emily Dickinson wrote to a friend, "You cannot imagine how trying they are, because if we

Emily Dickinson

cannot go through them all in a specified time, we are sent home." She added, "I never would endure the suspense which I endured during those three days again for all the treasures in the world." Emily compared notes with her brother, Austin, a student at Amherst College, and discovered that her courses and exams were just as difficult as his.

To the students who got through the entrance exams and began their studies at Mount Holyoke, Mary passed along her lifelong enthusiasm for teaching. Great numbers of young women went on from Mount Holyoke to become teachers, some in difficult frontier areas. These young women followed Mary Lyon's stirring words: "Go where no one else is willing to go—do what no one else is willing to do!"

She also encouraged her students to teach "for the common good" rather than for money alone. Even as the head of Mount Holyoke, she herself would never accept more than two hundred dollars a year in salary. And all her life she gave a large part of her savings to religious missions.

Word of the success of Mount Holyoke graduates spread fast and far. But in spite of its success, Mary was not completely satisfied with Mount Holyoke Female Seminary. She wanted to change to a four-year course of study, as many men's colleges were doing. She also wanted to add more subjects and more classes. Her goal was to make the curriculum just as demanding as that of the men's colleges. How else could women become a power for good?

Members of the
Class of 1851

In February 1849, after caring for a sick student, Mary herself became seriously ill. Both students and teachers were at Mary's bedside day and night. On March 5, just after her fifty-second birthday, she died. She was buried on the campus that was her only home.

How did a poor unknown farm girl like Mary Lyon accomplish so much in such a short lifetime? Her old friend, Professor Hitchcock, said that once Mary saw there was a job to be done, she just couldn't wait to start. She couldn't bear to waste one minute of time.

Said one friend of Mary, "A good picture of her could never have been taken, for it would have been impossible to catch the vivacity of her face." This daguerreotype, an early kind of photograph, was taken on a day when 48-year-old Mary was not at her best.

Perhaps Mary realized her days on earth would scarcely be long enough. But she managed to change forever the education of women. In founding Mount Holyoke, she sent a signal to the world that women could and should be well educated.

"My heart has so yearned over the adult female youth in the common walks of life," she wrote in a letter to Hannah White, "…that it does seem to me that something more ought to be done and something more can be done."

The fire in Mary Lyon's bones burned just long enough for her to get "something more" done.

Afterword

At the laying of the cornerstone on October 3, 1836, Mary Lyon predicted that "this will be an era in female education. The work will not stop with this institution." History has proven her right. In 1893 her school became Mount Holyoke College. One hundred years after that, Mary Lyon was chosen as a member of the Women's Hall of Fame in Seneca Falls, New York.

Mary Lyon was a pioneer in establishing schools for women, but was she really fighting for "women's rights"? The phrase would probably have amused her. She saw no need to waste time proving that women had good minds. To her, that fact was just plain common sense. "It is the mark of a weak mind to be continually comparing the sexes and...making out the female sex as something great and superior."

Mary Lyon had the vision to see how women's education in the early nineteenth century could and should be improved. The lack of qualified teachers in the schoolrooms of the young United States meant that children were growing up ignorant. Mary had the drive and the energy to educate women to change all that.

This two-cent stamp was issued on February 28, 1987, in honor of Mary Lyon's 150th birthday. The stamp is colored Mount Holyoke blue.

By lowering costs, she put education in the reach of young women like herself who were poor but had good minds. By starting a permanent school, she made sure that people would take women's education just as seriously as they did education for men. And she ensured that young women would no longer be discouraged by having their school disappear in midcourse.

It would certainly delight Mary Lyon if she could see what her female seminary looks like today. The beautiful hilly campus is dotted with buildings: classrooms, laboratories, libraries, dormitories, an art center, a spiritual center, a gymnasium, and a swimming pool. Young women come to Mount Holyoke College from all over the country and all over the world to learn and to share in Mary's dream.

Notes

page 7

Biographies written not long after Mary Lyon's death report that her cousins loved telling the story of Mary and the hourglass. Nobody today knows if the hourglass story really happened. But everyone who knew Mary agreed that she never wasted a minute.

page 33

It was unusual for a young woman from a poor family to enroll in a private academy. Most of the young women who attended schools like Amherst Academy came from well-to-do families.

page 38

Many female academies failed when pupils were attracted because of the outstanding personality of the founder. If the founder left the school to go elsewhere, students no longer came and the school soon had to close.

page 51

It is puzzling that not one of Mary's letters contains a mention of this romantic episode in her life. Possibly her friends who later copied her letters deliberately left out some parts. Perhaps they thought such personal matters were not for the public eye.

page 60

Fund-raising for Mary's school became Roswell Hawks's life-work. He continued to do it for twenty years after Mount Holyoke opened.

page 62

A dormitory on campus today is called Safford Hall after Deacon and Mrs. Safford.

page 64

Andrew Porter's name lives on today both as a dormitory and as a favorite steamed pudding, called "Deacon Porter's Hat," served at Mount Holyoke College.

page 64

After seeing the cornerstone laid, Mary wrote, "The stone & brick & mortar speak a language, which vibrates through my very soul .... This will be an era in female education. The work will not stop with this institution. The enterprise may have to struggle...for years, but its influence will be felt."

page 69

One of the young men from the village hired to help move in furniture was so smitten by one of the students that a romance bloomed. Nancy Everett and John Dwight of South Hadley eventually married.

page 75

Emily Dickinson is considered one of our finest poets. Much has been made of the fact that she spent only one year at Mount Holyoke. However, not staying for the full three years was common at that time, especially for girls who did not intend to teach. About Mary Lyon, Emily wrote, "One thing is certain & that is that Miss Lyon & all the other teachers seem to consult our comfort & happiness in everything they do & you know that is pleasant."

Bibliography

Books:

Bianchi, Martha Dickinson. *The Life and Letters of Emily Dickinson.* New York: Biblo and Tannen, 1971.

Bingham, Millicent Todd. *Emily Dickinson's Home: The Early Years.* New York: Dover Publications, 1967.

Ferlazzo, Paul J. *Emily Dickinson.* Boston: Twayne Publishers, 1976.

Fisk, Fidelia. *Recollections of Mary Lyon, with Selections from Her Instructions to the Pupils in Mt. Holyoke Female Seminary.* Boston: American Tract Society, 1866.

Gilchrist, Beth Bradford. *The Life of Mary Lyon.* Boston: Houghton Mifflin, 1910.

Green, Elizabeth Alden. *Mary Lyon and Mount Holyoke: Opening the Gates.* Hanover, NH: University Press of New England, 1979.

Hitchcock, Edward. *The Power of Christian Benevolence Illustrated in the Life and Labor of Mary Lyon.* Northampton, MA: Bridgman and Childs, 1858.

Howe, M. A. De Wolfe. *Classic Shades: Five Leaders of Learning and Their Colleges.* Boston: Little, Brown, 1928.

Johnson, Thomas H., editor. *The Letters of Emily Dickinson.* Cambridge, MA: Harvard University Press, 1965.

Mount Holyoke College. *The Centenary of Mount Holyoke College.* South Hadley, MA: Mount Holyoke College, 1937.

Mount Holyoke Female Seminary. *Memorial: Twenty-Fifth Anniversary of the Mt. Holyoke Female Seminary.* South Hadley, MA: Mount Holyoke Female Seminary, 1862.

Stow, Sarah D. Locke. *History of Mount Holyoke Seminary, South Hadley, Mass. , during the First Half Century, 1837–1887.* South Hadley, MA: Mount Holyoke Female Seminary, 1887.

Articles:

Browne, Sheila E. "Daring to Dream—Women Scientists Then and Now." *Mount Holyoke Alumnae Quarterly* LXXVI (Winter 1993).

Duffy, Joan R. "A Thread of Faith—Mary Lyon's Missionary Vision." *Mount Holyoke Alumnae Quarterly* LXXVI (Summer 1992).

Gass, Marilyn Talbot. "Preparing Leaders in Education—A Mount Holyoke Tradition." *Mount Holyoke Alumnae Quarterly* LXXVI (Fall 1992).

Hooker, Henrietta Edgecomb. "Mount Holyoke College, South Hadley, Mass." Offprint. *New England Magazine* 15 (January 1897).

Infantini, Father Joseph, Rev. Katharine Baker-Carr, and Rabbi Carolyn Braun. "Spiritual Life at Mount Holyoke." *Mount Holyoke Alumnae Quarterly* LXXVI (Summer 1992).

McFeely, William S. "Mary Lyon: The Life of Her Mind." *Mount Holyoke Alumnae Quarterly* LXX (Winter 1987).

Wells, Anna Mary. "Emily Dickinson, 1849." *Mount Holyoke Alumnae Quarterly* LXX (Spring 1986).

All quotations in this biography were taken from the above sources.

$\mathcal{I}$ndex

Illustrations are reproduced through the courtesy of: Mount Holyoke College Library/ Archives, front and back covers (all), pp. 16, 37, 46, 50, 61, 62, 64, 67, 68, 73, 74, 77, 78; Mills College Library, Special Collections, p. 2; Mount Holyoke College Art Museum, South Hadley, MA, pp. 6 (*Mary Lyon's Birthplace,* detail, Edwin Romanzo Elmer), 63 (*3rd Meeting House, South Hadley,* Joseph Goodhue Chandler, gift of Mrs. Thomas E. Brown, Jr.), 70 (*Nancy Everett Dwight and Melatiah,* detail, Joseph Goodhue Chandler, gift of the legatees of the estate of Katharine Dwight Berry); Buckland Historical Society, Buckland, MA, p. 9; Museum of American Textile History, p. 11; Library of Congress, pp. 14, 24; The Society for the Preservation of New England Antiquities, pp. 20 (both), 36 (photography by George Noyes), 39, 45; Ashfield Historical Society, Ashfield, MA, pp. 28, 29; The Jones Library, Inc., Amherst, MA, p. 33; Amherst College Archives, pp. 40, 41; Laura Westlund, The Lerner Group, p. 48; Ipswich Historical Society, Ipswich, MA, pp. 53, 59; *American Scenery,* W. H. Bartlett/IPS, p. 56; Amherst College Library, p. 75; Copyrighted stamp design reproduced with permission of the U.S. Postal Service, p. 81; Dorothy Schack Rosen, on her graduation from Mount Holyoke College, p. 88.

About the Author

Dorothy Schack Rosen, pictured at the time of her graduation from Mount Holyoke College, has long been fascinated by the school's founder, Mary Lyon. Mrs. Rosen is a children's librarian and a teacher of English as an International Language. With her husband, Sidney, she is also the author of several murder mysteries and two novels for young readers, *The Baghdad Mission* and *The Magician's Apprentice,* both published by Carolrhoda Books. *A Fire in Her Bones* is Dorothy Rosen's first biography for children.